BEFOREHAND

BEFOREHAND

John Marshall

Ekstasis Editions

Canadian Cataloguing in Publication Data

Marshall, John,
    Beforehand

    Poems
    ISBN 1-896860-38-9

        I. Title.
    PS8576.A757B43   1998   C811'.54   C98-911070-2
    PR9199.3.M382B43   1998

© John Marshall 1998.
All rights reserved.

ACKNOWLEDGEMENTS:
Some of these poems were originally published in the following periodicals: *Canadian Literature*, *CV 2*, *Fiddlehead*, *Grain*, *Prairie Fire*, *Malahat Review*.

Published in 1998 by:
Ekstasis Editions Canada Ltd.
Box 8474, Main Postal Outlet
Victoria, B.C. V8W 3S1

Ekstasis Editions
Box 571
Banff, Alberta T0L 0C0

THE CANADA COUNCIL | LE CONSEIL DES ARTS
FOR THE ARTS | DU CANADA
SINCE 1957 | DEPUIS 1957

Beforehand has been published with the assistance of a grant from the Canada Council and the Cultural Services Branch of British Columbia.

For Emily, Andrew, Beverley,
Jesse, and Grace Marshall

CONTENTS

I

Deaf Mute Dreamer

Sargo, Talking / 13
1956 / 15
Harewood / 17
Southend / 20
Ghost / 21
Beguiled / 23
Chance Memory / 25
The Weight / 26
The Gift / 28
Stepsons / 31

II

Broken Islands

"stone" / 37
"it's the old mouth above" / 38
"quiet tide of heaven" / 39
"claws for earth" / 40
"nudge" / 41
"snout of something being eaten" / 42
"light takes on" / 43
"the little bigger eat the small" / 44
"algebra of friendship" / 45
"driftwood crawls rain-scored rock" / 46

III

Substitute Love

Earth Rising / 49
Denman / 51
Names of Trees & Letters / 59
Mackey Maclaren / 63
Friends / 64
Two Cities & A Town / 65
Beforehand / 67
Notes For Rhododendron / 68
Postcard / 70
The Traveller / 71
Master / 73
Natural Dream Lexicon / 74
Found Poem / 76

*And now and then a son, a daughter, hears it
now and then a son, a daughter,
gets away*

Lew Welch

I

Deaf Mute Dreamer

Sargo, Talking

Falling back of Bute Inlet then
you should have seen the trees ten twelve foot through
and straight
it made you stop and think sometimes
they went side by side as far as you could see
it was beautiful timber.
Them days you'd work with a partner

and we'd got along good over the years
never no problems
worked hard worked fast
made sure we got our money.
The part of it is

he was just bucking ends at the landing
helping out
giving them a hand at the end of the day
when the pile shifts
and a log crusht him
just like that.
He didn't even die right then

but by the time I crawled through to him
I could see he couldn't live.
So there he is

hung up
the log pressing all the blood back up
to his heart.
I mean the first aid had to tell him

more or less he was dead
all that was keeping him alive
was the log.
Wasn't much to say

asked him does he want me to say something
you know to the wife and kids
but there wasn't nothing to say.
I rolled him a smoke

but he couldn't really draw on it.
All he says is what the hell

cut it.
We knew what happened when it went cut through
and me I'm the one did it.
He died like that

that's how he was killed
it all sort of just went out of him.
I took that smoke from his lips

finished the goddamned thing myself.
I don't think a week's gone by thirty years

I don't think of it.
I tell you John
he was a good man.
Don't you never do no work

where you need a partner.

1956

1904 West 16th Avenue
first address I ever had

sent from the float-camp
somewhere in Knight Inlet
to Cypress House Private School
a handful at five.

1904 West 16th Avenue
the first address I had
to memorize so I memorized
where I was lost.

The first class the first day is ballet
and I'm already inclined to say goddamn
or bullshit or both

can't stop laughing in those mirrors
all of us dressed in the same dumb blue

and when I am asked to hold out one hand
after the other hand to be hurt I am trying
to remember what I look like
in water.

That school was something that needed
to be run away from
and from the first firedrill on
I planned a route

I would live alone
in the playhouse somehow
at the edge of the grounds.

Weekends most everyone goes home
I say now I lay me
but stay awake

pull another sweater
over the sound of my heart

and when I am reaching for the panic bar
I know I have found my way
to the secret door.

It was cold
by the time I was found.

And how they treat you
different after you've run away.

But that night in the playhouse
I dreamed of my mother
she was sending my clothes far away on a line
and the line went on into the sky off the edge
of the floats
and the sun was close
falling through the thin worn parts
of her housedress onto me

and though I called and called

I did not know her name

Harewood

for Ken Cathers

remember where the mountain was in the sky
before the mountain is money
I remember the morning fluorescent ribbons
materialized the fields

remember our names as they were called
through cupped hands
we were always far enough away
to claim we couldn't hear

remember how we'd get hell for it
our being late their worry
but some days wouldn't end even
and how we learned to make our breath silent
to better play dead in those fields

remember looking back and the shapes
our bodies left in the grass
the grass lifted them back
in the air each blade
lifted us back in air

I remember wondering are we that light
and how excited I was to read
my first book about angels
also how disappointed I was
not in the pictures

remember how we told time
evergreens gone violet in sunset
how I want to remember the beauty
of that time

remember the not-wanting and wanting
to go home and knowing all the way
who lived in every house
I remember their names now

remember where you were known as love
love they called you every day
remember whatever story
it was you told
was it fishing for surgeons
whatever it was every time you told it
what laughter they laughed how dear
we must have been even then to them

I remember what it was
I wanted to remember
we found that bell in the muck by the stream
and we kept it we kept moving it
to more and more secret places
until we forgot
all about it

do you remember
is it hidden there a memorial
a perfection of its place and its finding
and where would we go now
in search of it

all the cows are long gone
fences gone the sheds fallen in
the cedars of the barn were gone silver
back then remember how slippery
they were to climb
and it was a little dangerous
but we climbed it anyway
as children always do
against what they are told

why was there some distance or view
we wanted to take on or in or was it
just to give ourselves something
to remember ourselves by

and what if we can't remember
what if we can not find the courage now
if only to pull ourselves away
from all we've let die in us

do you remember that day we decided
to become men
we were only children
our parents had a certain pride in our lives
and we stood in the air we had climbed
and we decided to remember
what it all was
where everything was

I call us on that pact we made
I remember what it was we saw that day
it was our last glimpse
of the dust of the sea

Southend

for Karen Lane

In the wood and mills then
somebody's old man was always coming home
all busted up maybe just short something.

For us kids
making our way from school
it was a kind of competition
and it was certainly our end of town.

Outsiders had to
exhume grandfathers who went into the mines
or come up with an uncle
who fell in to the circles of water
did he did he really he did so

rich with bloody accidents
we fought ourselves over.

But it is no subject
and writing about it
a cruelty to all
who rushed those fears
safely home to her

and the stories we told
themselves
finally silencing us

what we simply lived with
become too much to follow.

Ghost

Hawk.
A child's rendition,
the wings and head good,
the body flying a problem.

What the real was was always
tearing itself in two, the light Blue
crayon for sky, Indigo

water. And you
you could still say this hawk
reads the water

but we are the water
when we are not looking up
piecing off the light
with a thing or two.
Deus ex machina, prompt
one more alphabet—
it all gets dedicated to.

Another dead language
is learned for the dark
and though it is nothing
in itself it works well enough
in here in rooms
where insect lives are proofed.

Why for the benefit and for all
the generations of pure research

though it pays to join
and fill in memberships
in organizations

some will save the whales
from us.

Who remembers
even a few animals
from their marks
from childhood
before the glare was white
and the world was white
for all its colors
and we drew out of it prophesizing
our small abstract.

Beguiled

He was being read to pictures
the day it left the page
he went looking for it in the green after
the top foot of water.

"A little farther on, they passed a Tiger"

she reads, he plays blind
the breath-shapes light on his face. Except
the invisible words
she breathed in. Imaginary

sounds. He couldn't tell which
one was most like the other.

The frog showed up pinned open
the little heart-thing still beat
he fed a drop of caffeine in
and made notes observing.

All fall carcasses hung
where the car is parked.
Methodically dressed,
head off
the hides were always saved
for the Fish & Game.
They walked

in practiced silence,
it was like second nature.
With her

the sky was on top of itself.

Further on
he drop-folds
in cardboard boxes
all the clothes of the dead
sent off to the Goodwill. Again.

Everything emptied out equally.

Rain.

Words were like words were
I said in the day or the night
but in the dreams
they were live.

And where words were said to be born
to stand in for water and to lie
agreeably between earth and sky
like the little deaths they are

the kills of a reflected forgotten paradise.

And I was one
of the deaf mute dreamers
who drew blue lines across a page
to stop the sky.

Chance Memory

Go ahead
it's the one someone meant to
take of you as a child,
the only one ever taken
of you alone.

You are at a tree
or with water
or under the shadow
of something extraordinary
men have made.

In that picture
everyone loves because you look happy
only you see the sky
in the black and the white
where the blue slipped in,
or a sound swept by so close
your smile went wide.

You must not mind being thought a fool
to look for that here
now we have been all the way to the moon
and elsewhere and proved
nothing is missing
inside us.

It is there
it was always there
it never left you

it does not know how to leave you.

I can't tell us apart.

The Weight

God at ten pounds a week a month
passes fast.
Grown amazed at herself she
calls it the *perfect*
diet though a *little*
extreme.
The aside is

(see)
your teeth
don't fit.
She suggests she's become
an extra for some operatic production

or better yet an understudy she'd stress
by now *sotto voce*

being perfectly bald.

And refusing a wig out of vanity
wears a florid pink on yellow
bathcap *lively*

aren't they
fingering what passed for flowers.

Pretty much silence after.

The chemicals.

The cauliflower black flesh
blossoming up from her groin.
What
stripped her of her

courage. It was killing.
And he was so young he was reading
What Is Existentialism?

and by the illumination of the machinery
slept long nights in what he believed
was a chair.

The Gift

It's the end of this life
and every day after
free of the
or from the twin terminals

or of a past and the future.
But surprised at times
by the fierce pain a heat
so white so quick it's
a confusion of this life
and the

to come.
Although the drugs float you up
you ask him all the time
to come closer
"I'm right here"

"I know"

How scared was I knowing
one of the nights
I sat with a knife
strangled in my palm.
I didn't know

how to help
you what was
I going to do
little fool
release the blue cords at our wrists

for us both.
No
that was for me
my own love I couldn't stand
the end of.

She let me go
as with all other things
waving me away
from my great distance beside her

though how we held on
it was the closer part again
we couldn't get any closer.

Lost even her hand
in the terrible sleep
in the killed head.

And sit with a body
left to what remains
of its ruined wisdom.

She stops
a moment
and with all I know I think this is still impossible
but the moment lasts

and I
am breathing in the gentlest air
I am breathing in
a child's breath

I kissed her then

it was her last gift to me

opening my burnt eyes

I saw a woman
for the first time in my life.

Stepsons

We walk the aisles of caskets
followed respectfully
by the undertaker our guide
what's he afraid of
shoplifters

impatient with the role
he's going to leave us
alone with our decision

but we are left
because we are a hard sell
and because behind the sad music background
chimes reveal new customers.

They all would have heard my brother say
what a bunch of bullshit

> and it is your voice I hear
> clear in his own
> and all I see is winter
> the evenings after work
> the little wooden rowboat
> graceful on sawhorses

all of our lives you were giving us something
with your hands.

We both stand stupid
before the luxurious

the permanently reverential sounds
from unseen speakers
a cheapness to match the tastefully
hidden image of christ repeated
in the carpet pattern.

We stand stupid
before the law in this country

we can't touch you
now you are some thing
worry will we
over what you will wear
will we dress you in a suit
you never wore once
in your life

and which to choose of these
ornaments lit to display
will attest to our
love
is it.

We opt for a plain box

the resident of the funeral home
naturally tries one more mean voice
you being a poor sale
which is what you are most

but we learned the hard way
how to turn harder
you taught us what that is
out of your life

it is no strength
but on occasion useful
for dealing with such as these
who work grief to advantage
who would try to sell us unlimited
expression of what
our own sentiments
please is it thank you
not too bloody likely.

We are without manners

by the time we leave he's forgotten
to remember our first names
calls us sir.

And what we feel most is empty but
weirdly elated.

In the parking lot
we can't remember how a car works
we sat there
two full grown men

sons and daughters of our own at school and at home

and wept and laughed together
like children.

II

Broken Islands

for Lorraine Martinuik

[1]

stone
and the surround of stone

all that is known
of sand, of myth-like

infant light

but it has always been
necessary to imagine sky

imagine even to keep the sun
even

and what colored stones
if stone could be
put together
would make beautifully
a gravestone

and what patterns what letters
would water unlock

but
who lives so long

as to tell

[2]

it's the old mouth above
et cetera but god

but what roots
what end

if an arm can be made out
amputated from light

and the plunge of bodies
between this slap of space:

and overall: the completely
concentric crack of sun

[3]

quiet tide of heaven

rock half-bent by water
some darkness

in stone stone
whatever air

pushes through
to air

still rock water

beneath it all, sand-colored
slow graph of stars

[4]

claws for earth

amid rock and air, whitening
out, skeletal

half-eaten
and longing, longing

never far
from what made it swell
bends over water
into water itself

then the big wind and the breaking
away and being tossed up

who hopes understands
the empty nest of roots in air
and the terrible light

become terrible above

[5]

nudge
of whales

a mother pushes
her young to air

and this
older, more scarred
one afloat
over rock the rock
cuts and cuts

and the young rest
confident upon the endless body
of life bleeding and healing and

is there water for all this
red to run into

[6]

snout of something being eaten
inside and out

almost see air
sharpening itself

the light collapsing black

decay's pattern
against the long life of rock

an organ, even a heart
would look much like this

would so worn by the pact
bleed the white page, ironically

to its dot

[7]

light takes on
the creased face of rock
and suns itself
content

[8]

the little bigger eat the small

it's a permanent strain, it's petrified
and it blesses us all

who go tongue to tongue
to service ceremoniously

great black
and great stone

[9]

algebra of friendship

lichen whitens squared figures
of rock

fern spreads the knot-hole

all branches of the world,
with a wind
negative against it all

and who have run now rest
have given over to other forms of life

everywhere else
an endless

idiot
silence

[10]

driftwood crawls rain-scored rock
and aims a riot of mouths
at water and at air

bull-kelp sails in the foreground,
a line of light caught dark

we await
a tide

a lifetime

and wonder which
generation that is

of birds
overhead

III

Substitute Love

Earth Rising

The last of the alder leaves
have caught in the branches
of the young red maple.

Snow started over an hour ago
the tires are still under the bed
with the christmas decorations.

Soon it will be a problem.
Snow's a form of remembering in
a thoughtful way. But like water

the waves can't really be looked at.
There's the same harmlessness
to it. Like a walk

taken in squared circles
and further and further from the house,
began to think there is no weather

wherever you are. No north
wind drives the birds south.
Some other home.

Maybe it's just
the quiet of everything
being made equal.

The afternoon already wasted
reading the new philosophy,
which when translated I think means

fuck you.
A civilization down to
two word propositions.

This far west
it's always a shootout
cogito vs. intelligo.

But to report that
after the hard rains
the earth sends up stone

for the moon to sun on.
You have to have
sat for days

squaring the light
with the window
for that.

A few trees,
their weight down
to shadows.

It's all getting settled.
And it's the little more,
tonight, and that's all—

no, that's not all,
it's the knowing
first thing in the morning

the horses will act crazy.

Denman

[1]

Cougar
Coal
Waterloo

Rosewall
the creeks, bridges
on our way home

Cougar, Coal, Waterloo, Rosewall—
it's a memory game we play
then they make up the words of a song

we sing to where we are,
taking turns
with what comes next,

with the order of what we know,
epistemology at 60—
Big Qualicum

the impossible rhyme stumps us
but Little Qualicum comes along—
the signs nearly too small

for the words—and we start the river songs
rivers this close to the end of
rivers, and so it goes on, and we

father and daughter
following our own
starfish directions.

[2]

I was coming back here from cities
traveling with a woman who painted
the weather in light.

I was always coming back here
before you were born.
Watch the dawn colors

worn round the point.
All huge, hard
to hold onto—

as the wind whitens
the water the little farther
evidence of the outer

spaces the shore.
Mark after mark
inspired by all

which has come before.
The constant revising the current
forms which world

is afterwards named.
But the mysteries
do remain.

Shells,
shells you found with tiny holes
to pass a thread through.

[3]

Our lives,
coincide.
This necklace

you made
and gave away.
Where I've kept stones

cups of sky, sea-blue.
Hands
are pools.

(And one day you fall
safely in love, your lips
meet the depths

what is briefly and beyond
for us all). A
parenthesis hope

is without end
part of the circle, a stone
we send glances

the water. And in my own way
I can see how far we go
we go across bare frames

in the wide-open
of love and light,
reading

one moment
to next
over this precipice.

[4]

Fourteen years ago
the same long grass slope
cabin to sea-cliff

where birds were
leaves wind lifted
back into birds.

I couldn't figure out
the clouds
from the shore.

[5]

You draw a heart
off-center
in the starfish we traced.

I'll be 36 this year
I've been standing at a post
eyes closed, counting, for years.

I'd add lists of events
of a kind—but
only relations hold

the complex. The relation
of memory itself is seen
too parallel a tactic.

So, whatever you follow
follow for the love of it.
Live, everything lives out time,

and imagine, a body which out lives
the body, life going on
driven by the heart you have drawn.

[6]

Back at the cabin,
blue windows.
You gather the things

you keep close to your life
a kiss, and you're off to bed.
Back at the beach

I was going to call you back
to see what remained of a fawn,
its future an intricate vertebrae arc.

Had it stumbled and become
strange to itself
as it fell the cliff-face? Did it

see the shadow,
its shadow, as for the first time
really a belonging

of the sky
and have this shadow seem separately to be
falling back up the cliff to grass-safety?

Who knows,
vision is fast
is in its trying-to-be

something like life
seems appropriately
about to surprise itself

back into itself, but
exhausted by what it has attempted
falls unable even to comfort itself.

Hope it didn't
have to lay with that little
enough we are sometimes given,

enough to keep the heart going
but that's all
and the eyes, little clouds, staring

at all it had in the sun seconds
ago been.
Or maybe it just followed its mother,

drowned trying to cross Lambert Channel.
Maybe its father paused
dumbfounded, where he stood

and saw, indifferently, the slow strangeness
of two single heads
and the water, the familiar

bobbing for a body.
Face it,
it's likely it died at birth.

But I am thankful
you didn't ask for a story tonight
the why and why and why

the beautiful constant
poem of asking of the world
what it can be.

Stay, stare
one last night,
before the window

the window where the stars are
the bones of what we listen in
for what's more.

The Names of Trees & Letters

A faller,
after the high rigging is finished
winters works high steel in cities.
But one winter

when the wind came
and the snow came
you stayed in camp.
"Watchman" you wrote

alone through the snows
christmas I remember that christmas
the piles of presents the money made
you must have been living on nothing
that winter you stayed
watching the cold machines
making sure everything
didn't freeze up.
Not exactly your kind of job

but that winter started
with Phelps' funeral,
and you wouldn't leave the one place on earth
you'd kept waking up in

knowing that we guessed
how alone it was you had to be.
It was the second time in your life

you wrote a few letters, those others
to your mother when a child
in North Africa during a war.
She liked to remember by saying you got into that war

telling the only lie she knew of
your whole life.
How our love will

attach certain fondness to memory,
the fixed creation
inverse proportions
to what time destroys.
He'd left the farm in Shipman at twelve

to work the bush on the coast
sending twenty dollars a month home
kept his sisters in school,
what else he could spare
brought his brothers out.
They were working the bush the fields the weeds

they were men who took on the size of what they did,
friends who work there now call it the jungle,
after too much vietnam tv.
After the war he went back to what he knew

tougher than ever on everyone,
fired one brother twice one season
pick up your jam can
no explanation necessary.
Although the story Bill loved most

told they were both children
cutting wood miles from home in Saskatchewan—
he'd near cut off a pair of toes
trying to keep up

and you put him on your shoulder and ran
mile after mile
and there was a little snow all the way
home where she always was
with her needle and thread,
her coal oil.
Your brothers and sisters

they all had their stories and they all
made me wonder when it was
you got to be a child.
My mother said you always sat with your back

to the walls in bars
the kind of man who made enemies
of those who crept up from behind.

He was a careful man although
killed by accident.
At the funeral in Victoria
we went through the crowd
who couldn't get in—
it was like the lineups I stood in
to see movies in Nanaimo.
I sat next to your second wife

a namesake I remember I steadied her
when she was unable to stand alone at the end
a child within months of being born inside her.

So what you taught me
ends with tucking in my shirt

and that day in the woods
what was it you had to show me
telling me all the names of the trees
I already knew

and which tree in which season
where the pitch would be—
what you shut two of my fingers so firmly together
with the other hand I could not pull them apart.

It's the end of February again
cold wind and the magic of snow
falls from the moon over Saskatchewan.
His body a cold machine of the earth
underground twenty-nine years. His mother
lived twelve years beyond him.
I've reached

for those letters for thirty years—
I've reached the age you were
killed and I must find my own way
to keep alive imagining
your birthdays. Today I was

splitting the wood I buy—
humming the song already sung,
I found my hands shone

and you   began to talk   but
it was too sudden   I couldn't lift my eyes
from my own huge hands
I was pushing   the pitch   rolling it off

our hands
here   the blood stopped.

I near fell down
and a little burst,
uncontrollable, of laughter—
to think you were some kind of naturalist first.
To think what the truth might be

our hands
and what we've measured by them.

All else are silent days I have come a little close to you
and all the rest of my life lived miraculously apart.

Mackey Maclaren

Everyone phoning looking for you, now you've
gone. Are they afraid you'll show up at the door
after they've answered, something extinct
live in your hands.
Letters ask after your health arriving
as though delayed in some far world.
And the women of children you might have had
file constant moral claims, their hands
are still in your hair.
I've already received paper from the stock
romantics, who will try on any death
if it will further elaborate their fit
to shadows.
There's the odd polite complaint
about how far you pushed the experimental.
And let's face it, you never could type worth shit.
I haven't heard from so many friends
since the year I gave all my books away.

Friends

Drain a bottle of vodka like a pop.
Heart just stops. That's
if you're man enough

not to puke. That's
question begging. Pull
the trigger, imagine

your head won't explode.
Some just walk
in the blank

water.
Cures
for this grief

walk around the house
until you can go in.
Inside open and close the doors.

And throw rocks in water.

Go on throw rocks in water.
Say your own name,
over and over.

Two Cities & A Town

Bill's last night last night
4 a.m. again
                DirTy Jesus
I feel rough

usually wasn't sleeping much.

Never hear him
get an extra
syllable in beautiful
again.
It's the Saskatchewan.

Not on fire

anymore, is he, no. No
more Jack Daniels. No more pills
left over from a war.

No more half-years
so far out of it it'd be civilized

to call it the bush.

No more dead brother's face
breathing in mirrors.

I went looking
for the Paradise Club
where he was the bouncer once
threw everyone
sober out.

And an overpass rose
cars onto planes.

There's heaven
history for you.

What to do with winter.

Which elevator door
opens first.
We'd bet
finally on anything. *How*

get out of this life.

It's the year's collect.

Beforehand

I remember you
as a child
to be sure
I say our secret
without seeing
the red figures
I know
they're there
as the sound slides
like light unnoticed
before the mirror
was a mirror
I drew our faces
in clouds where
our breath caught
we were this close
we were touching
I loved you
then as a child
loves not knowing
what it is

Notes For Rhododendron

Monday ten new ones
and every week a test.
They start off

with spelling bees
arms landing craft
and make some strange noises.
They're left with rhododendron

a word they decide
should be forced to spell itself.
I am piqued he says and adamantly
falsetto it helps.
Space it out and it sounds

like a sentence
rho do den dron.
It did she asks

questioning the equivalence
translation: she wishes to know
which is the verb do or dron.
They have work to do

if everything is to be gotten right by Friday.

He watches her fingertip
traces in air

she touches silence writing

erases immediately a mistake
with her palm.

And he's told *don't look*

she's seven and she can tell
what disappears

from what is invisible.

And who taught her the alphabet

learns with each season
how time has likewise fallen
secretly in with space.

They practice
repeating to remember
letter after letter

and when he surprises her with hyacinth
a word out of order

she presses her eyes close

maybe to see one
like the ones they planted together
last fall.

Like the way we sometimes do

to remember each other.

Postcard

Picture Tate Giacomettis

"it's like i've never seen before

*they are so far away
and are they ever alone*

*but they are like the spaces
that close between waves*

*as when we once loved
to swim in the darkness*

*and raced each other
to the shore"*

16 years later
she mails the card back
no note no nothing

why she saved it why
I've saved little

the skin does crawl
this lifesize

this small.
Maybe it's Space &

Time she's telling me.
Are we even now.
Dear Elizabeth.

All I ever loved
bathes in silence.

The Traveller

for Douwe Stuurman

Santa Barbara sirens run the aqueduct
from the dam to the mission,
the sign reads the indians
built it under supervision.

At the Botanical Gardens
we take turns talking to trees.
At a doubled redwood trunk
he quotes a man of virtue
out of the blue. Frail,
he's near aerial—

    what you will love most

is to walk
on the earth

and he makes you drive
to meadows
to walk. To where
the wild meadows were.
He wants you to see everything.

Sitting, he's near silent
but up and about you get Reed in the thirties
Huxley, Krishnamurti,
what Solvang was like before the tourist machine.
His near-anonymous report

of one man's half-century
reading Proust.

And if one of your stories is well told
the praise is in saying
it sounds like you've begun

to love to know.

And when you leave
he presses a cloth bag
of wildflower seeds
in your other hand.

He'd gone into the Gift Shop
that day you thought you were waiting
while he had a piss.

Now you remember the way you felt.
Your stepfather slipping you
an extra twenty
to help you on your way
when it was time to leave.

And how they left their hands in ours
that split second longer

gave us all we needed.

Master

for Bob Lane

Some days later
I followed my dog up Harewood Road
past all the houses and beyond the last fences
of the few farms left.
I walked past the dam then took the powerline shortcut
to walk above the river
before going down into the brush
surrounding the edges of First Lake.
I found him there dead.
But at 18, what a life
a kind of glory in the length of that life
even dead.

I had found him in the place
I went to every chance I got
and from the banks
to the darkest holes
drew gold eyes of rainbows up
and out of the surface
that was the magnet
broken and broken
fished for it again and again
never once coming back thought
I had caught enough.

And that dog
he would hardly ever be around
I barely remember him here
until it was time to leave
and he would reappear
and we would walk this way back to where we lived
exhilarated by where we had been.

Natural Dream Lexicon

She's called out of the dark
she's proud she's no longer afraid of

surprised to see she's made herself
so small.
She was on a picnic with her mother
something like men
but all hairy too like beasts
captured us and we're put in their cage
and we are frightened but we get a chance to escape
and we do escape but we've been in the cage
for three weeks and we are very hungry
and we decide to eat berries but we can't remember
and we eat the wrong berries and we get sick
and we're too sick to run away anymore
and they find us and put us back in the cage
what is scary is
they want to eat us
and there's nothing we can do
but they can't eat us because they see how sick we are
so they let us go

so we go straight back home

Strange to forget
how homesick it is to feel and think
of what it is she sees to say.
He won't fool you into believing

anything he can do can help,
nor choose among the little lies of assent
and find his excuse in them.

A little girl visiting Dad
lets him leave the light on awhile.
From the zoo posters they try
lion   rhinoceros   tiger
it makes them feel better to see
they are not afraid of what they say.
They talk some of those other creatures

also on the wall
which no one alive has ever seen.
She is satisfied

they will not hide
from what they have said.

He will look in on her later

and later in her life.

Found Poem

Emily's

My		Book	Ho		ANot Abat
					Wat I Hav
cigaM			esu		Bin Doing
Gard					I Patad
					Today
	ne				Ysdrday

He lettered My
in huge blue crayon,
the mystery
at about three.
ANot is hers
in a delicate pencil,
we figure she was four.
It's an old care —
I tell her,
to write a facing page.
No point in repeating
the not-writing in books part.
And leaving off
the thirty odd years
gone somewhere.
Then she shows him
how to close the book
so that their hands
always touch.

Printed in November 1998 by

in Boucherville, Quebec